Wham, What a Mess!

By Cameron Macintosh

Shaz was up on a big box in the shed.

"Chip!" yelled Shaz. "Come and get this chess set."

When Chip set off,
he whizzed into a big pot.

Chip's top bit fell off!

Chum ran up to Chip.

"Chip, where are you?"
said Shaz.

"Chip is not well,"
yelled Chum. "I will come."

But Chum whizzed into
a lamp!

Thud!

Then Chum's leg fell off!

Then Chip ran into Chum.

Wham! Hiss!

"What a mess!" said Chum.

Shaz ran in.

'What a **big** mess!"
she said. "I will fix this."

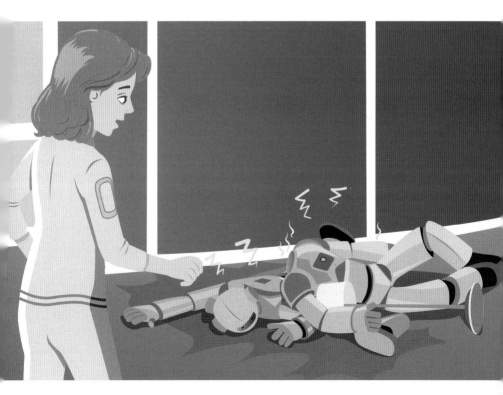

Shaz got her kit in the shed.

Shaz put Chip's top bit on.

Then she put Chum's leg on.

They all went to the shed.

Chip and Chum went up
and got the chess set.

CHECKING FOR MEANING

1. What happened to Chip when he whizzed into the big pot? *(Literal)*

2. Why did Chum's leg fall off? *(Literal)*

3. Why were Chip and Chum able to get the chess set? *(Inferential)*

EXTENDING VOCABULARY

whizzed	When Chip and Chum *whizzed,* how did they move? Was it fast or slow? Can you think of any other words that have the same meaning as *whizzed*?
wham	*Wham* is an example of onomatopoeia. Can you remember what this word means? What other words in the text are examples of onomatopoeia?
mess	What is a *mess*? Have you ever made a mess? What were you doing? Did you have to tidy up your mess?

MOVING BEYOND THE TEXT

1. What is chess? What do you need to play chess?

2. What games do you like to play? Who plays them with you? What do you need to play these games?

3. If you had a robot, what jobs would you like it to do for you? Why?

4. What tools do people keep in a tool kit? What can you fix with tools?

SPEED SOUNDS

| sh | ch | th | th | wh | qu | ph |

voiced   unvoiced

PRACTICE WORDS

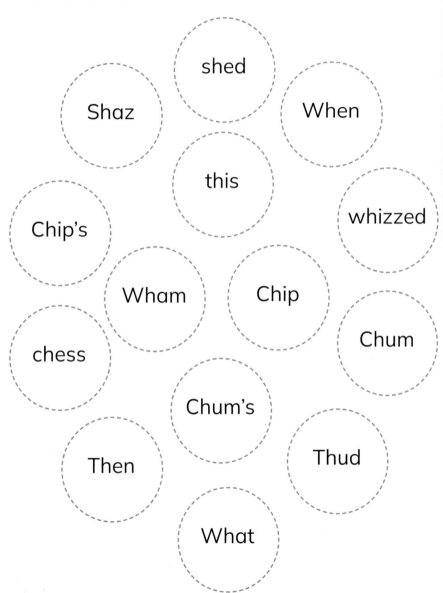

shed

Shaz

When

this

Chip's

whizzed

Wham

Chip

chess

Chum

Chum's

Then

Thud

What